Voting Guidelines for Christians

By Larry J. Tate

Bible Translations

All scripture quotations are taken from the
Holy Bible, King James Version,
Cambridge, 1769. Used by permission. All
rights reserved.

Table of Contents

Introduction

Voting is the method our Country's citizens utilize as the right to make decisions regarding the direction our Country should go. The United States of America was established on Christian principles, and the Constitution ensures that we have the opportunity for those Christian principles to continue. This is accomplished by our right to vote.

The United States is a Republic, which means that the citizens have supreme power. The citizens of this Country are entitled to vote for officers and representatives who are in turn, responsible to us. We are a government by the people, not by a monarchy, and not by a dictator. The governing statutes, laws, and policies are established through the representatives we place in office.

Most Judges are appointed to office by elected representatives, such as a Governor, or the President of the United States. The few remaining judgeships are chosen by the results of an election. The duty of a judge is to interpret the intent of already-established law and then enforce that interpretation. The problem with interpreting of the law, is that a liberal-leaning, activist judge can alter the original intent of the law, or worse yet, create a new law.

If we want this Country to follow Christian values, it is our responsibility to elect representatives who will enact laws that are consistent with Christian standards. It is our responsibility to ensure that our representatives appoint judges who will interpret those laws from a conservative point of view.

There are nearly as many questions about voting as there are voters. Is it necessary to vote? Does my one little vote count? What difference does it make? Do I really have any business influencing the direction our Country is taking? Am I acting as if I'm God when I vote? Doesn't God have control of the direction this world is taking? And if so, why should I take the risk of going against God's will? This book will help you find answers to all of these questions.

America's New Direction

America has come to a fork in the road. The road to the right supports Christian values. The road to the left embraces humanistic and ungodly values. We have veered to the left, and if we continue in that direction, this great Country of ours will no longer be recognizable.

Political Correctness has become the standard by which we live. Out of fear that we could offend even a single person, we talk, we act, and we advertise our products with *inclusiveness* in mind. Political Correctness has closed the door to speaking our mind. Political Correctness is eliminating the aspect of being an individual with personal ideals, and forcing us to think and act in such a manner as to prevent the possibility of offending anyone else.

Homosexuality has taken this Country by storm. Not only have we approved homosexual marriage, we as a Country now applaud and endorse that particular lifestyle. Even in cases where a statewide vote of the people has ruled against homosexual marriage, the courts have intervened and ruled that the will of the people is unconstitutional. If we dare say anything negative about that particular subculture, we are labeled as homophobes. Homosexual relationships have become so common that same-sex couples can now adopt children as easily as traditionally-married people.

Transgender people are coming out of the woodwork. Not only are some people changing their gender by operations, a larger number are simply choosing to pretend to be the other gender without actually going through the surgical operation. The politically correct environment has made room for this lifestyle by permitting men to use ladies locker rooms, and allowing ladies to utilize the men's facilities. Sex education at our public schools has taken a sharp turn to the left as well. Now, our children are being taught that homosexuality and the transgender lifestyle is not only to be tolerated, but it is to be embraced and celebrated.

The institution of marriage is being attacked from every angle. Divorce is now as simple as changing jobs. Single parenting is now the norm, not the exception. The new norm is for people to simply live together and raise children. Then when they decide to break up, they simply enter into another relationship, with little to no concern over the welfare of the children.

Birth control pills which were once common methods for preventing a pregnancy, are now being replaced with abortion pills, or morning-after pills. The humanistic government we are subjected to is now making it possible for children to purchase birth control products without the consent or knowledge of their parents. Abortion is now a common solution for birth control. Rather than going to a doctor to end an unwanted pregnancy, women go to assembly-line abortion clinics. Abortion is no longer considered by our government to be the act of ending a child's life. Instead, it is simply viewed as a woman's right to exercise control of her own body. The child inside her body is considered to be little more than so much biological tissue.

Often times, abortions are justified by practitioners by pointing to the benefits of embryonic stem cell research that will assist in the health of people, when in actuality, this stem cell research is merely a weak excuse for not only continuing the practice of abortions, but to increase the brutal practice.

God is being removed from the public sphere at an alarming rate. Atheism and humanism is the driving force behind the removal of God from the public square. Public meetings are banning prayers that include the name of Jesus. Instead, prayers are of such a generic nature that they end up being inclusive of all religions. The moment of silence is quickly replacing any prayer at all. The Ten Commandments are being removed from public property at an alarming rate. Separation of Church and State is at the tip of every liberal tongue. While Christianity is being suppressed and put down, other religions, especially Islam are being uplifted and praised.

Children are being prohibited from praying at school. Prayer at high school graduations is disappearing. The theory of evolution is being touted as if it is a hard fact while creationism is being declared as nothing but religious silliness.

Saying "Merry Christmas" is quickly becoming a violation of political correctness. The Christmas holiday is being replaced with a Winter holiday. Christmas trees are becoming known as Gift trees. Easter break is becoming the Spring break. In spite of the fact that America is mostly Christian, we cannot celebrate Christmas the way we want to, for fear of offending Muslims, Buddhists, Secularists, and Atheists.

Illegal Aliens are praised for breaking the law. A cashless society is around the corner. A One World Government is being discussed. All of these things are taking us down the pathway to the Mark of the Beast.

It seems odd that the belief system of the majority of our citizens is not in line with the direction that this Country is taking. It seems odd that the belief system of the majority of our citizens is not allowed to be displayed in public areas.

In April, 2013, President Obama addressed Planned Parenthood. Speaking of abortion, he said that there were those who want to roll back women's basic rights to the 1950's. Basic rights? It's incredulous to think that the killing of unborn children could be classified as a basic right. Then, he ended his speech by saying, "Thank you, Planned Parenthood. God bless you."

Really? God bless Planned Parenthood? This is an organization, funded in no small part by the United States government, which performs about 1,000 abortions per day.

We would never expect to hear our president say, "God bless our nation's rapists," or "God bless our thieves and robbers," or "God bless the murderers across this great land of ours," but "God bless Planned Parenthood" is apparently fine and dandy.

In so many words, what our president really said was, "God bless irresponsibility," and "God bless debauchery." We have ushered in a time when the pursuit of pleasure trumps responsibility. We as a nation are telling our children that they can do whatever they want to do because there are no consequences for irresponsible behavior. Our nation's moral compass is spinning out of control. It's high time we wake up before it's too late.

For a thorough examination of the rise of these and other societal changes, read "Shadow Truth" by Larry Tate.

Christians speak out about America's Debauchery

If America is anything, it is diverse. However, one thing that links most Americans together, is Jesus Christ. A whopping eighty-three percent of Americans identify themselves as Christians.[1] Fifty-three percent of Americans are Protestants. Thirty-seven percent of all Christians describe themselves as born-again evangelicals.

If there is anything we can be sure of, it's that Jesus does not approve of abortion as a method of birth control. All life is precious to Jesus, even that of an unborn child. To some degree, even certain aspects of U.S. law agrees with that. If a person does harm to a pregnant lady, and such harm ends up killing her unborn child, that perpetrator will be accused of committing murder.

God's plan is that a man and a woman would become one flesh by way of marriage. The uniting of a man with a man, or a woman with a woman was never looked on favorably in the Word of God. Consequently, our Savior is not a supporter of homosexual marriage.

If Jesus is anything, he certainly is not politically correct. Look at the way he chastised the Pharisees. Look at the way he refused to participate in the traditional washing of hands when he visited the home of a Pharisee. Look at the name-calling he utilized when speaking to the Pharisees.

Since eighty-three percent of Americans align themselves with Jesus, it is simple enough to deduct that the vast majority of Americans should share in the values that Jesus has. And sure enough, if you spend enough time around the typical American Christian, you will get an earful of complaints about the downward trend of this Country. Everywhere you go, you will hear Christians complaining about the decline in America's values.

"This Country is going downhill fast," they say. "Why are abortions so abundant? Why has homosexual marriage been legalized against the will of people? Why is political correctness preventing us from letting our Christian lights shine? Why are transgender people allowed to use whatever locker room and whatever restroom they desire? We in the majority do not approve of children being able to obtain birth control products without the consent of their parents, so why have the courts gone against the will of the people?"

"Why are the Ten Commandments being removed from our Courthouse lawns? We Christians represent the majority, but the minority is somehow ruling over us. Why is that? How is that? If we want to say 'Merry Christmas,' we should be able to do so. Why are we being forced to wish our customers 'Happy Holidays' when we are at work? Why is prayer being removed from our school functions? If we as the majority wish to say a prayer at a high school graduation, we should be allowed to do so."

"Where did all of these liberal judges and liberal courts come from? How dare they rule against the will of the people? Judges and courts are creating new legislation that goes against Christian values. For one thing, that is the responsibility of Congress, not the courts. For another thing, this is a Country that is supposed to adhere to the will of the people. How can they rule against our wishes? The decisions being made by the Supreme Court are tearing the fabric of this Country apart."

There can be little doubt that America's Christian population is in a quandary as to why they are being subjected to rules, regulations, laws, and court decisions that are contrary to the beliefs of the majority of the population. America is in a downward spiral in spite of the fact that the majority portion of the populace claims to have no part in that downward trend.

Whose Fault is it?

If you spend enough time around fellow Christians, you will hear complaints about the debauchery of America, and plenty more. They have a valid point. If eighty-three percent of Americans are Christians, there should be no way that laws, rules, regulations and court decisions could go against us. And yet, they do. Something is very, very wrong with this picture. What can it possibly be?

The answer is simple, and at the same time, it is an indictment. The American democratic process assures that the will of the people is to be the law of the land. Since eighty-three percent of Americans profess to be of the Christian faith, there should be no question as to how our laws should be set up. We may not like the answer, but the Christian community as a whole, is responsible for the mess we've found ourselves in!

America's laws are established by representatives we have elected to office. Our judges have been appointed by Governors and Presidents we have placed in office. The people we willingly chose to represent our interests are the very people who have created the judicial rulings that we so love to hate. Our representatives were chosen in the voting booth. The will of the Christian majority is absolutely and completely responsible for the decline of our moral code. The Christian vote is the very action that has caused the decline of America's moral compass.

Yes, a good number of Christians *do* vote for the right candidates, but it is quite obvious that most do not. For one reason or another, many Christians forget their Christian values when they enter the voting booth and select the candidates who do not support the Christian point of view.

Another reason why this Country is going downhill has to do with the fact that far too many Christians are so apathetic that they don't even bother to get out of their easy chairs and cast their ballots. Instead, they would rather sit in front of their TV's, listen to all that's wrong with America, and complain about the downward spiral we are in. Their indignant self-righteousness allows them to blame everyone else for the state of this Country's morals, but they refuse to acknowledge that they are the very ones who are responsible for the conditions they so love to hate. So-called conservatives love to complain about how our leaders are going against the will of the citizens. But what are they actually doing about it? Many Christians don't bother to vote at all. Most of those who *do* vote, vote only in the General Election, while staying away from the Primaries. Fewer still, vote in the State elections where the Governor and State lawmakers are selected. Finally, a very small percentage of America's Christians have the incentive to vote in the County, Local, and School elections.

As for those who *do* bother to vote, how do you suppose they make their decisions? Most voting decisions have more to do with personalities of the candidates, the physical appearance of the candidates, or certain highlights gleaned from the evening news. Very few Christian voters consider all of the values of a candidate. Very few Christian voters take the time to consider a candidate's position on abortion, homosexual marriage, God in the Public Square, etc. Very few Christian voters have considered whether or not a candidate is socially conservative or not. Instead, most Christian voters make up their minds according to conversations heard around the water-cooler.

The sad and simple answer as to why eighty-three percent of the American population allows our Country to descend into a downward spiral can be boiled down to just one word: apathy. The silent majority is apathetic regarding issues and elections. The silent majority is grossly apathetic regarding the issues of abortion, homosexuality, transgender life styles, political correctness, and a host of other sinful issues. As a matter of fact, the "silent" portion of "silent majority" is a sin in and of itself. America's Christian majority wears a cloak of Christian beliefs and values, but they are lacking in real substance. America's Christian majority is not living out the beliefs they claim to have on the inside.

Suppose that a stranger were to approach you with an offer of a substantial income for the rest of your life?

Chances are, you would ask the stranger if there was a catch to his offer. As you suspect, everything in life has certain consequences. The stranger says he has only three things you must do. You must deny Jesus and abandon all of your morals. You must promote the homosexual agenda to every person you meet. And finally, you must publicly encourage the practice of having abortions for the purpose of birth control. That's all there is to it. If you would devote every waking moment to promoting those three things, you would be assured of income for life. If you're like most Americans, you would tell the stranger to keep his money. You would never deny Jesus and sacrifice your morals, not even for a lifetime of income.

You may not be willing to sacrifice your own morals, but apparently many of the people in this Country are doing that very thing. If it were not so, we would not be subjected to the laws that are going against Christian values. If it were not so, activist judges would not be re-shaping this great Country of ours. In spite of the fact that the majority of this Country claims to be conservative Christians, the majority opinion no longer seems to count. It just takes a small panel of judges, or in many cases, even a single judge, to strike down the wishes of that majority.

Liberal judges are at war with the Ten Commandments. The Ten Commandments are being banned from public property left and right. In the year 2015, the Supreme Court went against the wishes of the majority and struck down the laws of every state that had previously banned homosexual marriage. With one fell swoop, a panel consisting of only nine judges used their power and authority to overrule the will of the people. Thirdly, abortion has become as simple as a desire and a choice to be made by pregnant women.

Often times, we Christians are prone to say, "It was a panel of judges that made those leftist decisions. I have no control over what they do. The judges have been appointed by leftist politicians, and there isn't a thing I can do about it."

That is exactly what the left wants you to think. They want you to believe that you are powerless when it comes to the direction this Country is heading. Sadly though, if you think you have no say in the laws that are being passed, and if you think you have no say in the decisions made by activist judges, you are wrong—very, very, wrong.

In reality, a significant number of conservative Christian Americans are taking the stranger's offer without even realizing it. How are they doing it? They're doing it in the voting booth. In this Country, the majority still rules. Every politician wins his office by garnering a majority vote. Even judges are placed in their positions by the majority. There are two ways for a judge to gain power. He must be elected, or he must be appointed. If elected, the judge wins his judgeship by way of a majority vote. If appointed by a politician, the politician who did the appointing won his position by way of a majority vote. Consequently, every policy and every law in this country has the backing of the majority of the electorate.

"This can't be," you may say. "Every person I meet is offended by the laws and decisions being handed down by our politicians and judges. The majority of this Country is conservative. "

The simple fact is—the conservative majority is directly responsible for every one of the decisions made by this Country's leftist judges. The conservative majority is apparently too greedy and uninterested to do anything about it. The problem lies with the fact that most conservative voters go to the voting booth without having done their homework, that is, if they bother going to the voting booth at all. Thinking they are just voting on a few high-profile candidates, when they get to the voting booth, they find confusing state questions and decisions about the re-appointment of certain unknown judges. What do they do? It's like a multiple choice exam where a student hasn't put forth the effort to study properly. On a random basis, they check "yes" on some questions, and "no" on others, not even considering the fact that they are making critical decisions about where this Country is heading. Just as shocking, they sometimes ignore those portions of the ballot altogether.

If a conservative voter was truly responsible, he or she would make an effort to obtain a copy of the ballot long before voting day, and then make an informed decision about every single choice that needs to be made. State questions and judgeships should be researched, and voting choices should be decided accordingly.

What should you do when faced with voting for, or against judges you've never heard of? Like any student at school, you should study. What sort of record does that particular judge have? What political party are they affiliated with? Who—and this is very important—who first appointed this judge? Was the judge appointed by a liberal governor? If so, this judge is likely to make liberal decisions.

"What about the Supreme Court?" you may say. "We, the people, have absolutely no say in those appointments. The President of the United States usually appoints those high-profile judgeships. We are left completely out of the loop."

Quite to the contrary, you the conservative majority, have a lot to do with Supreme Court appointments. If you voted for the President who did the appointing, then you are directly responsible for his appointments to the Supreme Court.

"But I voted for that President because of his stand on financial issues. I needed financial help with Food Stamps, Welfare, Union representation at work, Entitlements, and financial help for the lower class. Yes, I wanted his fiscal agenda. I wasn't necessarily impressed with his social agenda, but in order to obtain the financial help I so desperately needed, I had no choice but to swallow hard, and vote for him anyway."

There you go. Your vote traded a politician's promise of more money and financial support for this nation's downward slide into immorality. You, the "conservative" Christian took the stranger's offer of money in exchange for a decline into immorality.

There's no such thing as claiming that the people have no responsibility for a judge's immoral and ungodly decisions. Every voter has the right and responsibility of determining which direction this Country is heading.

Back to the premise of this chapter: Who's to blame for this Country's moral decline? We are quick to proclaim that America is a Christian nation. Therefore, by simple logic, the professing Christians of this nation are responsible for its moral decline.

Let's assume that the majority of America is still Christian, and the majority of Americans still love God, and they walk with God on a daily basis. How then, can we as conservative Christians change the direction we are heading? Even if we have financial needs that the politicians are promising to fix, we should consider their financial promises last—not first. If we want this Country to regain the greatness it once had, the first thing we should consider, is the politician's stand on social issues, along with his walk with God. Then, and only then, should we consider his stand on financial issues. If we as a nation will ignore our greed, and stand up for what's right, we can reverse the downward slide that is taking us into a state of oblivion.

Matthew 5:16 says it all. *"Let your light so shine before men, that they may see your good works, and glorify your Father which is in heaven."* This passage reminds us of the children's gospel song, "This little light of mine." We are not to hide our light from the world. Rather, we are obligated to let our light shine. It is time for conservative Christians to let their light shine rather than hiding it as if they are embarrassed about it.

Is America a Christian nation? Are there more Christians in America than non-Christians? The results of the nation's religious polls tell us that we are a Christian nation. However, our enacted laws, our judges' decisions, and our nation's practices tell us that we are anything *but* a Christian nation. The only logical conclusion is that many of our professing Christians are in fact, *imitation* Christians.

Some would protest, saying that perhaps many of the imitation Christians are to blame for the state this Country is in, but the *Evangelical* Christians are standing up for that which is right. Okay, let's look at it from that angle. It is true that of the evangelicals who *do* take the effort to vote are quite conservative. Approximately 80% of Evangelical voters cast their ballots for conservative candidates.[2]

However, that is only part of the statistics regarding Evangelicals. Now, brace yourself for the alarming numbers.

On average, 17% of registered Evangelical voters do not bother to get out of their easy chairs and vote. Another 19% of Evangelicals who are *eligible* to vote, never take the time to register to vote. This comes to a grand total of 36% of Evangelicals who do not vote even though they could if the wanted to.[3] Since Evangelicals historically vote for conservative candidates, this apathy on the part of more than one-third of all Evangelicals is responsible for much of the mess we as a nation find ourselves in.

What would it take to return this Country to greatness? It's simple. First, we need to return to an intimate walk with God. And secondly, we need to let our light shine. That's it. It is that simple.

Christian Responsibility for our Situation.

Behind every abortion being performed in America, is a Christian who decided to stay home on Election Day.

Standing in support of every homosexual marriage in America, is a Christian who is more interested in entitlements than in adhering to godly principles.

Rooting for policies that allow transgender persons to have access to whichever locker room they choose, is a Christian who was too lazy to study the issues.

Offering a helping hand in every politically correct policy, is a Christian who did not vote in the Primary Elections.

Helping to promote the policy of handing out birth control pills to teenage girls without parental consent, is a Christian who voted for a Governor who promised more jobs, while at the same time, supporting anti-Christian values.

Encouraging a ban on prayer at high school graduations and other school functions, is a Christian who had better things to do than to vote at the School Board Election.

Assisting in the removal of the Ten Commandments from the courthouse lawn, is a Christian who expressed little-to-no interest in the election of his State Senators and Representatives.

Supporting the policy that prevents store employees from wishing customers "Merry Christmas," and instead offering the all-inclusive "Happy Holidays," is a Christian who wasn't even aware that the City and County elections were going on.

■ ■ ■

It is sad to say, but statistics prove that the voting habits of America's self-professed Christians are responsible for the rapid decline in America's value system.

Would you spit on the Bible?

There is a sad story of martyrdom in a distant land. In an effort to quash a rise in Christian belief, a group of soldiers marched into a church and instructed the members of the church that if they did not want to die, they would have to spit on the Bible and deny the existence of God. All but one of the members complied with the soldiers' demands. When the last member made his way to the front of the church, he carefully wiped the spit off the Bible, and then prayed for God's mercy upon those who had already desecrated the Word of God. Seeing that the man was defying their demands, the soldiers shot him dead.

Ask any self-professed Christian if they would consider spitting on the Bible and denying God. With very few exceptions, they will tell you they would do as the martyred man did. Really? Would it surprise you to realize that many American Christians may be doing that very same thing with regularity? "No way," you may say, "no way." Continue reading and make up your own mind. They may not be literally spitting on the Bible, but what they are doing is just as much of an abomination.

There is a growing trend in America of expecting government-supplied financial support and safety nets. As a nation, we are looking for more welfare benefits, longer periods of unemployment compensation, more food stamps, higher minimum wages, education support, housing assistance, comfortable retirement income, and health care benefits for everyone.

Consequently, when many of America's "Christians" go to the voting booth, they pull the handle in favor of the politicians who promise to facilitate and enable such benefits and entitlements. The problem is…those financial safety nets have a very hefty price tag attached to them. Like many prescription medicines, the side effects may be worse than the cure.

Unfortunately, the financial aspect of these liberal programs happens to be joined at the hip with a sinister and evil moral aspect. The two cannot be separated. Why? Who knows? Humanism, which is inextricably intertwined with socialistic policies unashamedly denies the existence of God. Read the Humanist Manifesto I, II, and III to see just how anti-god this movement is.

Socialism is inherently contrary to godly principles. According to the humanistic aspect of Socialism and Communism, there is no God and therefore no Bible. There is no sin, and there are no morals, and there are no virtues with eternal values. Karl Marx, the father of the Socialism/Communism model, is attributed with saying, "Religion is the impotence of the human mind to deal with occurrences it cannot understand." He is also credited with saying, "The first requisite for happiness of the people is the abolition of religion." This mindset is bringing with it ideas, philosophies, actions and attitudes that will ultimately destroy our way of life.

As voters have allowed more and more financial safety nets to come to their aid, a devalued moral tide is also creeping in. The government and the courts began banning prayer at schools and removing references to Jesus, God, and the Ten Commandments from the public square. Abortion is common place, and contraceptives are now being handed out to teens without parental consent. Sex education classes in schools are beginning to cast homosexuality in a positive light, if not a preferential light. The family unit is being defragmented, and the Defense of Marriage Act has been declared unconstitutional by our President. Schools are beginning to avoid celebrating Thanksgiving, Christmas and Easter for fear that those Christian-oriented terms could possibly offend just one student who thinks otherwise. Instead, they promote Turkey day, Winter Holiday, and Spring Break. In the name of religious diversity, colleges are discouraging public displays related to Christianity, while at the same time, promoting anything related to Islam. The terms, civil liberty, separation of church and state, and political correctness are now common place. We are permitting the ACLU to get in the middle of everything we do.

All of this came along as part of the financial safety-net package we as a nation have been voting for. The majority of our nation professes to be Christian, so by default, self-proclaimed Christians permitted it to happen. Why? Because they voted for politicians who promised financial support, while at the same time downplaying the sinister aspect of their socialistic programs.

Christians know biblical truth, and they know the principles of God. In spite of that, we find ourselves, as a Christian nation, violating the laws of God, and heading in a direction that will eventually be disastrous for us, for our children, and for the generations that are to come unless we make up our minds to change the direction we are going.

The introduction of socialistic-styled programs is an attempt to destroy the Christian spirit in America. Now, socialistic philosophies are spreading across America like an infectious disease. American Capitalism has been the only force preventing the entire world from slipping into Socialism. When we eventually fall, the whole world will fall as well. Do you want this nation to keep going where it's going or do you want us to get back on track? America's future is on the line. Now is the time to speak up, stand up, and vote to save America!

Have you ever stopped long enough to consider the fact that your vote for government-provided financial support may be the same as spitting on the Bible and denying God? It's worth the effort to look around and see if it just may be true.

Who is Responsible for the Downfall of Civilization?

The downfall of civilization won't be the result of widespread abortion rates. It won't be due to the removal of God from our schools, courthouses and other public places. It won't have anything to do with our rapid decline in morality. The downfall of civilization won't be due to Socialism, entitlements, food stamps and dependency on big government. It won't have much to do with the decline of the family, children being raised by single parents or an outrageous divorce rate. The downfall of civilization will have little to do with corrupt left-wing politicians, lawmakers and activist judges. The above-mentioned problems are merely the symptoms of our impending downfall, not the root cause.

Who or what then, can possibly be responsible for the downfall of American civilization? The weight of the blame rests squarely on the shoulders of apathetic and low-information voting age citizens, the vast majority of which, are self-proclaimed Christians.

Our nation is comprised of an 83% Christian majority. Since we elect lawmakers and establish the laws of the land via a majority vote, simple logic tells us that a significant number of Christians are responsible for the current downward slide of our way of life.

Like an ostrich, the self-proclaimed "Christians" in America are hiding their heads in the sand, fooling themselves into thinking that if they cannot see a coming threat, then that danger will not materialize. Looking at only one side of a candidate's political platform, Christians are voting for liberal candidates who promise more entitlements, food stamps, welfare, extended unemployment benefits, higher minimum wages, and universal health care. As if they are blind in one eye, the Christians totally ignore the fact that the very same liberal candidates they are voting for, are also promising to remove God from public places, they are promising to promote an out-of-control abortion rate, and they are promising to celebrate homosexual marriage.

A large number of professing "Christians" are selling themselves out. Far too many professing "Christians" are making the decision to ignore the tenets of God's Word in exchange for an easier financial lifestyle. Go take a look in the mirror. Could you be one of those sell-outs?

Today's self-proclaimed "Christians" are doing the same thing that God's chosen people, the ancient Hebrews, did. The Hebrews chose to ignore the laws of God, thereby sending themselves into bondage. Today's self-proclaimed "Christians" are following the example that was established by the ancient Hebrews. They are ignoring God's moral laws by electing ungodly men to run our Country. Today's "Christians" are responsible for the downfall of this Country. It is sad to say that the actions of a good number of self-proclaimed "Christians" are in fact, proving that they are not truly Christian.

Legalized Bribery

Bribery is the act of offering money or other gifts with the intention of influencing the recipient in some way favorable to the party providing the bribe. Bribery is typically considered illegal and can be punishable by jail time.

There is no better example of recent political corruption than that of Governor Rod Blagojevich of Illinois, and his attempt to sell Barack Obama's vacated senatorial seat. This was a blatant attempt on Blagojevich's part to seek a bribe in return for the senatorial seat.

As Illinois Governor, he was afforded the final decision as to who would fill in then President-Elect Obama's empty Senate seat. The price for that Senate seat included such elements as a good salary for himself, a position for his wife on corporate boards where she would earn substantial amounts of money and an official position for himself as an ambassador.

As a result of his crime, the courts deemed him to be "unfit to serve," impeached him from his position as Illinois governor, and sentenced him to a fourteen year prison sentence. This is definitive evidence that the United States government considers bribery to be a serious crime.

Bribery is a crime unless it is the government that stands to benefit from the act of bribery. Then, it is okay. Our government is trending toward Socialism, and it will do anything, legal or illegal, to ensure the continuation of that trend. "No way," you may say, "the government can't be brazen enough to imprison individuals for offering and accepting bribes, while at the same time, being heavily involved in bribery itself."

Well sit tight and read on. For an example, let's take a look at the 2012 Democratic platform, and how the leaders of the Democratic Party dealt with Israel, God, homosexual marriage, and abortion.

The 2008 Democratic platform stated that Jerusalem "is and will remain" Israel's Capital. However, that particular line was removed from the 2012 Democratic platform. Only after a storm of criticism from Republicans and pro-Israel groups, did President Obama grudgingly direct the Democratic Party to amend its platform to restore language declaring Jerusalem as the Capital of Israel.

In 2012, Democrats omitted the word, "God" from their platform, a radical change from the party's 2008 document and a noticeable split from Republicans, who mentioned God ten times in their official party stance. Then, there is another matter. In 2009, while attempting to appease Muslim nations of the Middle East, President Obama declared to the country of Turkey, "We do not consider ourselves a Christian nation…we consider ourselves a nation of citizens who are bound by ideals and a set of values." There is an unending list of examples where our government is in the process of eliminating God from the public venue.

In 2012, the Democratic platform was altered to say, "We support marriage equality and support the movement to secure equal treatment under law for same-sex couples." In 2011, President Obama terminated the military's "Don't Ask, Don't Tell" policy, and in the same year, he decided not to enforce the Defense of Marriage Act which defined marriage as between a man and a woman.

The 2012 Democratic platform said, "Democrats will continue to stand up to Republican efforts to defund Planned Parenthood health centers. We oppose any and all efforts to weaken or undermine that right. Abortion is an intensely personal decision between a woman, her family, her doctor, and her clergy; there is no place for politicians or government to get in the way."

Abortion rights are difficult to understand. A woman can freely abort her unborn child for any reason, and that act is viewed by the government as a personal decision and a woman's right. Why? The government considers the unborn as no more than so much biological tissue. However, if someone were to injure that woman to the extent that her unborn child is killed, the government considers it murder. Why? In situations where someone injures a pregnant woman, the government considers the unborn child as just that—an unborn human being who has the right to life. It's strange how our government can change definitions to fit the whims of its leaders.

Okay, we see our liberal-leaning government denying God, throwing Israel to the dogs, promoting homosexual marriage and embracing abortion for any reason whatsoever. Here's the twist coming out of the twilight zone: virtually all of these practices are contrary to the Word of God—yet President Obama was easily returned to a second term of office! Approximately 83% of the American population claims to be Christian, and by default, *true* Christianity opposes these planks on the Democratic platform, but, the Democrats won anyway. How can that be?

Eighty-three percent of our voters claim to be Christian, yet 51% of all votes were in favor of the liberal candidate. It's time for a little math. Let's assume that all of the non-Christians voted for Obama (13% of all voters). That leaves only the Christian vote to be determined. Simple math tells us that the remaining 38% of the Obama vote came from professing "Christians."

Another alarming fact about the 2012 election is that 42.5% of eligible voters didn't even bother to get out of their easy chairs and vote. Since 83% of all Americans profess to be Christian, that is an awful large number of Christians who were so apathetic about the direction this Country is going, they didn't even bother to vote.

It's a whole lot more fun for these non-voting "Christians" to sit in their easy chairs and act righteous and judgmental about the direction this Country is going. What they fail to realize is that it is because of their own lack of voting that is contributing to that downward slide.

Those self-righteous Christians who sit in judgment are discussed by the Apostle Paul in the Book of Romans.

> [25] *Who changed the truth of God into a lie, and worshipped and served the creature more than the Creator, who is blessed for ever. Amen.* [26] *For this cause God gave them up unto vile affections: for even their women did change the natural use into that which is against nature:* [27] *And likewise also the men,*

leaving the natural use of the woman, burned in their lust one toward another; men with men working that which is unseemly, and receiving in themselves that recompence of their error which was meet. ²⁸And even as they did not like to retain God in their knowledge, God gave them over to a reprobate mind, to do those things which are not convenient; ²⁹Being filled with all unrighteousness, fornication, wickedness, covetousness, maliciousness; full of envy, murder, debate, deceit, malignity; whisperers, ³⁰Backbiters, haters of God, despiteful, proud, boasters, inventors of evil things, disobedient to parents, ³¹Without understanding, covenantbreakers, without natural affection, implacable, unmerciful: ³²Who knowing the judgment of God, that they which commit such things are worthy of death, not only do the same, but have pleasure in them that do them. ¹Therefore

> *thou art inexcusable, O man, whosoever thou*
> *art that judgest: for wherein thou judgest*
> *another, thou condemnest thyself; for thou*
> *that judgest doest the same things.*
> Romans 1:25-32 and Romans 2:1

The above passage is speaking of some of the very same conditions that are permeating our society today. Perhaps the non-voting Christians are not actually participating in those sins, but their lack of action at the voting booth is the same as doing those things. Romans 1:32 says that those who are judging are taking pleasure in those who are participating in the sin. The act of not voting is equivalent to taking pleasure in the decline of morality of this world.

There's a problem here. The statistics seem to suggest that a large segment of America's Christians support abandoning Israel, taking God out of the Democratic platform, supporting homosexual marriage, and permitting abortions at will. There are no two ways about it—a significant number of America's Christians ignored their core beliefs and voted for removing God from government, abandoning Israel, endorsing homosexual marriage, and aborting unborn children!

Why did nearly half of America's Christian citizens vote against their core beliefs? The answer may be shocking—the government offered a bribe, and a whole lot of Christians accepted that bribe.

It is a sad commentary on today's slide toward socialism, but our government is actively and overtly involved in bribery on a massive scale. Here are the facts: under President Obama's first term of office, the issuance of welfare checks, unemployment checks and food stamps skyrocketed. It even went so far that the possession of a cell phone was no longer considered a luxury, but a right. Consequently, our government began issuing free Obama Phones.

Our government is offering bribes for votes—and it is working magnificently. In exchange for easy qualification for welfare checks, unemployment benefits, food stamps, rewarding unwed mothers to have children out of wedlock, free cell phones, and other goodies, nearly half of America's

Christian citizens have chosen to ignore the non-Christian stance of the Democratic platform. Nearly half of the American Christian population is accepting the government's bribe and ignoring their Christian beliefs.

What is the penalty for being involved in this widespread bribe? The government certainly isn't going to send itself to jail. As for nearly half of the Christian voters, the government isn't going to send them to jail either.

The Bible talks about the wrongfulness of hiding our light under a bushel. Yet, when we vote for candidates who want to remove God from the public square, we are going directly against the Word of God. The Bible talks about blessing those who bless Israel and cursing those who curse Israel, but the Democratic platform is certainly trending the other way. The Bible teaches against homosexuality, but nearly half of all Christians are voting for candidates who take pleasure in homosexuality. The Bible teaches against murder, but a large number of Christians stand in support of killing unborn babies.

In summary, our government is bribing nearly half of America's Christians and those "Christians" are gleefully accepting the bribe. Sad to say, no one is going to jail.

Lazy, Apathetic Christians

Lazy, apathetic, judgmental, and disengaged "Christians" are paying little, if any, attention to the moral decline of America. They are quick to pass judgment on our Country's moral decline, but at the same time, they refuse to accept fault as to responsibility for that decline.

There are even some ministers who may be contributing to this situation more than they realize. From the pulpit they tend to steer away from any discussions that may be perceived to have political ramifications, and instead, tell their congregations that their job is simply to win souls for Christ. Continuing on, the ministers say that when people are won to the Lord, the moral decline of America will automatically decrease. They justify this statement by saying that converted Christians will follow the commands of God and lead morally upright lives. If this was the case, then the 83% of the American population that calls themselves Christian would have already taken care of that problem.

It is not as simple as winning souls to Christ. Both new and seasoned Christians should be indoctrinated in the commands of God. They should understand that they are not to merely sit in judgment of this Country's decline, but they should actively vote for the candidates who support Christian values. God's Word tells us to let our lights shine. We can let our lights shine in the voting booth as much as we can while walking down the street. Our light should broadcast the fact that Jesus became the supreme sacrifice of our sins, and that belief in him will assure our salvation. At the same time, our light should express a high moral compass. This can occur in the voting booth.

Being a Christian is much more than showing up on Sunday morning, singing a few songs, giving in the offering, and listening to a good, uplifting sermon. Being a Christian is an active task, and a burdensome task. God expects his followers to *do* something, not merely profess *to be* something. Many of America's Christians claim to be followers of Christ, but their actions loudly proclaim that they are anything *but,* Christian.

History Poised to Repeat Itself

Many of today's Christian voters are blindly contributing to the rising phase of liberalism. What they fail to realize, is that the assurance of promised financial security being offered by liberal politicians is little more than a ruse to enslave the very people who are allowing liberalism to come into power.

The United States was established by Christians who were escaping the bondage and regulations handed down by an oppressive government. Between Social Conservatism and a healthy dose of Capitalism, America went on to become the greatest and most prosperous nation on earth.

Today however, increasing numbers of Christian voters are choosing to elect leaders who are promising to provide entitlements, welfare, housing, health insurance, extended unemployment compensation, higher minimum wages, etc. These Christian voters justify this action by saying that Jesus was all about helping our neighbor in need, therefore, socialistic policies must be Christ-like. This is how Satan works. His deceitful ways are usually cloaked in a veil of truth. For detailed information about Satan's master plan, read, "Shadow Truth" by Larry J. Tate.

These liberal-voting Christians fall into one of two camps. In the first camp, is the apathetic Christian who has little to no interest in the direction this Country is heading. Yes, they love to complain about the social issues that are plaguing us, but somehow or another, they have taken themselves out of the equation that landed us in the mess we're in now.

In the second camp are the Christians who with eyes wide open, are voting for liberal candidates who have promised them financial aid, entitlements, etc. Even though there is always a social aspect and a financial aspect to each election, these Christians consider only the financial benefits that they are promised to reap. It is sad to say, that like an ostrich with its head in the sand, these same Christians are pretending not to understand that the price to be paid for the liberal candidates' promises of financial aid, is a systematic dismantling of Christianity. That is quite a price to pay for "helping our neighbor in need." As each new liberal leader is elected to office, more and more of our religious rights are being eliminated.

History has an uncanny knack for repeating itself. At the beginning of the nineteenth century, the Russian Empire was ruled by a Monarchy. While the Tsar lived in luxury, the general population of the country was living in poverty. In 1917, there was a revolution in which the Monarchy was overthrown, and a democratic form of government was established. There were several Parties seeking to be elected into the new government, and one of those Parties was the Russian Social Democratic Labor Party.

Because of promises of financial support for the people, the Bolshevik faction of the Russian Social Democratic Party rose to power. Once in power however, they began the process of implementing the concept of Communism and eliminating the democratic process that put them in their position. Along with implementing Communism, they forced atheism on the people.

Prior to the takeover of the government by Communists, the vast majority of the Russian people were religious believers. Once in control of government however, the Communists began destroying the beliefs of the very people who put them in power. Their aim was to break the power of religion and replace that belief with atheism. Science was espoused to be truth, and religious beliefs (such as Creationism) were cast in the light of only so much superstition. Religion was tolerated to a degree, in that people could get together in private. However, public displays of religion outside the church were prohibited. Due to the iron-fisted policy against religion, many church buildings were destroyed or converted to other uses.

The Communists utilized the seduction of financial aid to gain power. Consequently, Christians willingly allowed the Communists to govern them. Once in power however, the Communists systematically began dismantling anything and everything having to do with religious belief.

Today's American Christians have not learned from the lessons of history. We are following the examples established by the Soviets. Little by little, our government is removing the Ten Commandments from public properties, eliminating prayer in schools, etc. If allowed to continue, the United States will look more like Russia, and less like the great Country we once were.

The Prophecy Excuse

The Christians who don't vote are prone to say that their votes don't really matter because prophecy tells us that morals will decline, debauchery will increase, and the Mark of the Beast will take over the entire world. Somewhere in the midst of all this, will be the rapture of the Church.

"We have no business interfering with God's plan," say many of America's Christians. "God is in charge of all the rulers and kingdoms of the world. There is nothing we can do about it." One of the popular scriptures these Christians like to quote is Romans 13:1.

> *Let every soul be subject unto the higher powers. For there is no power but of God: the powers that be are ordained of God.*
> Romans 13:1

"As a matter of fact," they continue, "We are instructed that instead of being involved in the governmental process, we should simply pray for our rulers."

> *I exhort therefore, that, first of all, supplications, prayers, intercessions, and giving of thanks, be made for all men; For kings, and for all that are in authority; that we may lead a quiet and peaceable life in all godliness and honesty. For this is good and acceptable in the sight of God our Saviour;*
>
> I Timothy 2:1-3

Many Christians defend their silence on political issues by saying, "God did not call the Church to influence culture by way of legislation. What happens in this world is God's Will. We are to stay out of it. We should only pray that God's Will be done." They continue to say, "The Bible does not specifically instruct us to be involved in government, therefore, we should not voice our opinions in the voting booth. Instead of acting as if we are God, and trying to manipulate the direction of our government, we should simply pray for our leaders."

And finally, many non-voting Christians say, "The Great Commission instructs us that our duty is to win souls. Influencing the way our government operates is not found in the Great Commission."

> *Go ye therefore, and teach all nations,*
> *baptizing them in the name of the Father, and*
> *of the Son, and of the Holy Ghost:*
> Matthew 28:19.

Is the Prophecy Excuse Valid?

Non-voting Christians are quick to point out that prophecy tells us that a decline of morality is simply out of our control, and there is nothing we can do about it. Before accepting their weak and apathetic excuses, let's look at some Old Testament prophecies that had to do with ancient Israel being taken captive by other nations.

In the Old Testament days, the nation of Israel frequently fell into moral decline, and turned away from God. It was because of Israel's decline that the Lord sent a number prophets to warn them of the potential consequences of their choices. Jeremiah, Obadiah, Joel, Jonah, Amos, Hosea, Isaiah, Micah, Nahum, Zephaniah, Habakkuk, and others warned the people of Israel of the consequences of their sin, and pronounced God's judgment upon them. An example of this is found in the book of Hosea. Notice in this passage that God said that Israel destroyed itself. It did not suggest that

God was going to make them suffer whether they obeyed him or not.

> *² And now they sin more and more, and have made them molten images of their silver, and idols according to their own understanding, all of it the work of the craftsmen: they say of them, Let the men that sacrifice kiss the calves. ³ Therefore they shall be as the morning cloud and as the early dew that passeth away, as the chaff that is driven with the whirlwind out of the floor, and as the smoke out of the chimney. ⁴ Yet I am the LORD thy God from the land of Egypt, and thou shalt know no god but me: for there is no saviour beside me. ⁵ I did know thee in the wilderness, in the land of great drought. ⁶ According to their pasture, so were they filled; they were filled, and their heart was exalted; therefore have they forgotten me. ⁷ Therefore I will be unto them as a lion: as a*

*leopard by the way will I observe them: ^{8} I
will meet them as a bear that is bereaved of
her whelps, and will rend the caul of their
heart, and there will I devour them like a lion:
the wild beast shall tear them. ^{9} **O Israel,
thou hast destroyed thyself; but in me is
thine help.***

Hosea 13:2-9

Many Old Testament prophecies said that the nation of
Israel would soon be ravaged and destroyed by foreign
nations. The prophecies said that the inhabitants of Israel
would end up in a state of bondage to those wicked nations.
However, many of those prophecies also said that if Israel
would turn from its wicked ways, the nation would be
spared.

> ^{2} *The which Jeremiah the prophet spake unto
> all the people of Judah, and to all the
> inhabitants of Jerusalem, saying, ^{3} From the
> thirteenth year of Josiah the son of Amon king
> of Judah, even unto this day, that is the three*

and twentieth year, the word of the LORD hath come unto me, and I have spoken unto you, rising early and speaking; but **ye have not hearkened**. *4 And the* LORD *hath sent unto you all his servants the prophets, rising early and sending them; but* **ye have not hearkened***, nor inclined your ear to hear.* *5 They said, Turn ye again now every one from his evil way, and from the evil of your doings, and dwell in the land that the* LORD *hath given unto you and to your fathers for ever and ever:* *6 **And go not after other gods to serve them, and to worship them, and provoke me not to anger with the works of your hands; and I will do you no hurt.*** *7 Yet ye have not hearkened unto me, saith the* LORD*; that ye might provoke me to anger with the works of your hands to your own hurt.* *8 Therefore thus saith the* LORD *of hosts;* **Because ye have not heard my words,** *9 **Behold, I will send and take all the families*** *of the north, saith the* LORD, *and Nebuchadrezzar the king of Babylon, my servant, and will bring them against this land, and against the inhabitants thereof, and against all these nations round about, and will utterly destroy them, and make them an astonishment, and an hissing, and perpetual desolations.* [10] *Moreover I will take from them the voice of mirth, and the voice of gladness, the voice of the bridegroom, and the voice of the bride, the sound of the millstones, and the light of the candle.* [11] *And this whole land shall be a desolation, and an astonishment; and these nations shall serve the king of Babylon seventy years.*

Jeremiah 25:2-11

[21] *Go, enquire of the* LORD *for me, and for them that are left in Israel and in Judah, concerning the words of the book that is*

*found: **for great is the wrath of the Lord that is poured out upon us, because our fathers have not kept the word of the Lord**, to do after all that is written in this book.* ²² *And Hilkiah, and they that the king had appointed, went to Huldah the prophetess, the wife of Shallum the son of Tikvath, the son of Hasrah, keeper of the wardrobe; (now she dwelt in Jerusalem in the college:) and they spake to her to that effect.* ²³ *And she answered them, Thus saith the Lord God of Israel, Tell ye the man that sent you to me,* ²⁴ *Thus saith the Lord,* **Behold, I will bring evil upon this place, and upon the inhabitants thereof, even all the curses that are written in the book which they have read before the king of Judah:** ²⁵ **Because they have forsaken me, and have burned incense unto other gods, that they might provoke me to anger with all the works of their hands;**

therefore my wrath shall be poured out upon
this place, and shall not be quenched.

2 Chronicles 34:21-25

The people of Israel didn't listen to the prophets and continued to disobey God. As a result of their disobedience, God sent foreign nations to ravage the land and take its inhabitants into bondage. Keep in mind that the Old Testament prophecies regarding Israel being taken captive were due to Israel's failure to live in the manner in which God expected them to live.

The New Testament warned us that men's hearts will wax cold. This prophecy was not because the people have no choice in the matter. Instead, it had to do with the fact that many of today's "Christians" are making the conscious choice to allow that condition to happen.

> *[11] And many false prophets shall rise, and shall deceive many. [12] **And because iniquity shall abound,** the love of many shall wax cold. [13] But he that shall endure unto the end, the same shall be saved.*

Matt. 24:11-13

Another prophecy regarding the end of the Age is in 2nd
Thessalonians. You will see that like the Old Testament
prophecies, this one is also conditional. The condition is
regarding the falling away of mankind.

> *[1]Now we beseech you, brethren, by the*
> *coming of our Lord Jesus Christ, and by our*
> *gathering together unto him, [2] That ye be not*
> *soon shaken in mind, or be troubled, neither*
> *by spirit, nor by word, nor by letter as from*
> *us, as that the day of Christ is at hand. [3] Let*
> *no man deceive you by any means: **for that***
> ***day shall not come, except there come a***
> ***falling away first**, and that man of sin be*
> *revealed, the son of perdition;*
>
> 2 Thess. 2:1-3

If every Christian would live as God expects them to, they
would select good conservative leaders to govern them. If
Christians would be true Christians, Jesus would not have to
hasten his coming. Unfortunately, today's "Christians" say

that God's prophecy tells them that a great falling away will happen in spite of what they do, so their votes do not matter. Since today's "Christians" refuse to live as God expects them to, his prophesied coming will be sooner rather than later. The prophecies about the "falling away," the "Mark of the Beast," etc. have more to do with the deplorable spiritual condition of today's "Christians" than it does about a pre-determined plan of God. Today's "Christians" are refusing to learn from the errors of Ancient Israel.

Biblical Examples of Government Involvement by God's followers

Are we to stay out of our Country's political business? Should we forego the opportunity to inform our leaders of our opinions about the direction our Country is heading? Maybe this would be a good time to spend a little time looking at other scriptures in the Bible. Are there any instances in scripture where God's followers participated in government?

Joseph was involved in government. Not only was he involved, he actually participated as a government ruler.

> *And Pharaoh said unto Joseph, Forasmuch as God hath shewed thee all this, there is none so discreet and wise as thou art: Thou shalt be over my house, and according unto thy word shall all my people be ruled: only in the throne will I be greater than thou. And*

Pharaoh said unto Joseph, See, I have set thee over all the land of Egypt. And Pharaoh took off his ring from his hand, and put it upon Joseph's hand, and arrayed him in vestures of fine linen, and put a gold chain about his neck; And he made him to ride in the second chariot which he had; and they cried before him, Bow the knee: and he made him ruler over all the land of Egypt. And Pharaoh said unto Joseph, I am Pharaoh, and without thee shall no man lift up his hand or foot in all the land of Egypt.

Genesis 41:39-44

Another example of government involvement is found with Mordecai.

And Mordecai went out from the presence of the king in royal apparel of blue and white, and with a great crown of gold, and with a garment of fine linen and purple: and the city of Shushan rejoiced and was glad.

Esther 8:15

For Mordecai the Jew was next unto king Ahasuerus, and great among the Jews, and accepted of the multitude of his brethren, seeking the wealth of his people, and speaking peace to all his seed.

Esther 10:3

This is interesting. If God's followers are not to be involved in government processes, why was Joseph and Mordecai involved in government?

"Well, those examples are found in the Old Testament," some Christians may say. "What about the New Testament? The New Testament sets the stage for Christian activities."

Okay, let's consider someone in the New Testament who tampered with the leadership of the nation. John the Baptist wasn't afraid to offer his opinion to King Herod.

For John had said unto Herod, It is not lawful for thee to have thy brother's wife.

Mark 6:18

"That isn't a very good example," some "Christians" are inclined to say. "For one thing, it is only one example out of the whole New Testament. For another thing, John the Baptist lived prior to the Church age. Since the Bible is silent about Christian involvement in government, we should stay out of such affairs."

That may be a fair statement, so let's explore it a little further. What sort of governmental bodies existed in Bible times? Almost without exception, all governments were of an authoritarian sort. Generally, every country in the known world was ruled by a king, a monarch, a dictator or a pharaoh. In those kinds of governments, one or a handful of people were forcefully in charge of their subjects. There were no elections in those cases. If someone were to approach the king and tell him that he was running the country wrong, that person would likely be executed on the spot. In Jesus' day and in the days of the Apostles, the world's countries were still controlled by men who ruled by force.

As a consequence, the Bible was silent when it came to instructions regarding Christian involvement in government. "That's not fair," some may say. "If God wanted us to be involved in the direction of our Country, the Bible would have found some way to give us the proper instructions for such involvement. Besides that, all governments are put in place by God and ordained by God. We have no business interfering in God's plan."

Well, let's look a little closer. With that kind of logic, every modern-day Christian woman should be silent in the Church.

> *Let your women keep silence in the churches: for it is not permitted unto them to speak; but they are commanded to be under obedience as also saith the law. And if they will learn anything, let them ask their husbands at home: for **it is a shame for women to speak in the church.***
>
> I Corinthians 14:34-35.

In spite of this scripture, modern Christian women are far from silent in the Church. This seems to be a direct command, yet it is not obeyed in modern churches. Why? Perhaps it is because the position of women in Bible times was far different than the position of women in modern times. Times have changed and circumstances are different.

Then, there is the issue with slavery. Slavery was commonplace in both the Old Testament and the New Testament. There was nothing wrong with a Christian being a slave owner. Actually, it was quite normal. Consequently, there were rules that a Christian slave owner was obliged to adhere to. We 21st century Christians would never think of owning a slave just because the Apostle Paul thought it was just fine to own one.

> *Masters, give unto your servants that which*
> *is just and equal; knowing that ye also have*
> *a Master in heaven.*
> Colossians 4:1

The Bible says that governments were put in place by God. It stands to reason therefore, that the United States government was put in place by God. The Bible also says that we are to obey the government. According to Abraham Lincoln's Gettysburg Address, our government is, "...of the people, by the people, and for the people." The Preamble of the U.S. Constitution says, "We the People of the United States, in Order to form a more perfect Union, establish Justice, insure domestic Tranquility, provide for the common defence, promote the general Welfare, and secure the Blessings of Liberty to ourselves and our Posterity, do ordain and establish this Constitution for the United States of America."

The "of the people and by the people" in Lincoln's Address, and the "We the people" in the U.S. Constitution lets us know that all of the Country's citizens are by default, *obligated* to be involved in the direction our Country takes. As citizens of this great nation, we are *obliged* to have a voice in our government's affairs. This nation that was *"...ordained of God" (Romans 13:1),* was established to be ruled by the will of its citizens...not by the will of its leaders.

How often have we heard ministers remind us that we should thank God every day that we live in a free Country where we can say what we want, do what we want, read what we want and go where we want to go without fear of punishment from the government? How often have Christians expressed thankfulness that we can freely read our Bibles while at the same time, citizens of other countries are at risk of being jailed if they are caught with a Bible in their possession?

These freedoms did not come about by accident. Christian men formed this nation of freedoms. Ever since this nation was formed, voters have been electing people to office who have continued to keep our freedoms in place. In addition to electing people to office, a certain number of concerned citizens have reminded our leaders of the people's will. This is done by communicating with the leaders, either personally, by phone, or by mail.

Many Christians are quick to point out that our mission is to simply let our light shine before all of the unbelievers in the world, yet far too many Christians are not only apathetic when it comes to politics, they actually refuse to let their light shine when it comes to making their voices heard regarding the direction that our Country is heading.

There are two forces at work in this world, one evil and one righteous. Jesus said, *He that is not with me is against me, and he that gathered not with me scattereth abroad. Matthew 12:30.* By voting and communicating with our leaders, our nation goes in the direction its citizens instruct it to go. If Christians vote improperly, and if Christians don't vote, and if Christians don't communicate with our leaders, this nation will go the way of other nations of the world, which is away from God and away from God's principles.

Our Country was established on Judeo-Christian principles. However, that moral consensus has given way to many morally corrupt and hedonistic principles. This condition occurred only with the tacit approval of the Christian majority. How did the Christian majority approve such a change? They approved this change by way of their apathy. Instead of voicing their opposition to such changes, only a vast silence has been heard. The silence of many

Christians has also been evident at the polls. Sadly, less than half of self-described Christians voted in federal elections in the last fifty years. Too many voices within the Christian community are encouraging their fellow Christians to keep silent, especially when it comes to civic and cultural concerns.

The preservation of our freedom and morality depends on our citizens placing principled men in office. If we fail in this obligation, our government will soon be corrupted, and laws will be made that are not for the public good. Corrupt or incompetent men will end up being appointed to be judges, and the rights of our citizens will be violated or outright disregarded.

Americans are blessed with the freedom to organize, campaign, vote and write to their Senators and Congressmen. If they allow apathy to cause them to ignore that freedom, they may find themselves someday being held accountable for that apathy.

It seems reasonable that if Christians neglect their civil duty, they should not expect deliverance from the national consequences to follow. On the other hand, when Christians do the opposite, and diligently fulfill not just their duty toward God, but also their civic duty to their government, they will set the stage for His blessings on their land.

> [2] *When the righteous are in authority, the people rejoice: but when the wicked beareth rule, the people mourn.*
> Proverbs 29:2

> [34] *Righteousness exalteth a nation: but sin is a reproach to any people.*
> Proverbs 14:34.

Some Christians say that rather than voting and being otherwise involved in government, we should just obey I Timothy 2:1-2 which says that we should just pray for rulers. Continuing, they say that by being involved in the government, we might be working against God's power and plan to choose rulers according to His will.

> [1] *I exhort therefore, that, first of all, supplications, prayers, intercessions, and*

giving of thanks, be made for all men; [2] For
kings, and for all that are in authority; that
we may lead a quiet and peaceable life in all
godliness and honesty.
1 Tim. 2:1-2

Think on this for a moment. God instructs us in Matthew 6:11 to pray for our daily bread. Does this mean we should just sit back and let God do it all, or should we try to find a job and use that job as the means to obtain the answer to our prayer? Should we avoid looking for a job because we might take a job other than the one God in His providence wanted us to take?

[11] Give us this day our daily bread.
Matt. 6:11

In 3 John 2, the Apostle prays for believers' good health. Some people mistakenly believe that going to a doctor shows a lack of faith in God's power to answer prayer. Yet Christians know that the doctor may be the very means God uses to answer the prayer!

² Beloved, I wish above all things that thou mayest prosper and be in health, even as thy soul prospereth.

3 John 2

By default, all Americans are participants in political involvement. By participating, we have the opportunity of voting for our elected officials and for ensuring that we have proper and decent laws and traditions. If we truly believe our government was divinely ordained and instituted by God, this freedom and opportunity should not only be enjoyed, it should be exercised. By voting wrong, or by not voting, Christians are promoting an anti-God way of life.

Christians who vote, but are at the same time against writing to their Congressmen and Senators, may be confused. These Christians mistakenly say that voting is one thing, but writing to their leaders is meddling in God's plan. What then, is voting? Casting a vote can also be defined as meddling in God's plan. The very act of voting is the same as voicing one's opinions.

Christians should not be passive spectators in society's culture. While our primary task may the Great Commission, we are to engage our culture at all levels, advancing moral principles and seeking to restrain evil. Proverbs 29:2 clearly lets us know that Christian principles should be influencing our government, and if not, we will suffer.

> *2 When the righteous are in authority, the people rejoice: but when the wicked beareth rule, the people mourn.*
> Proverbs 29:2

Ezekiel 22:30 tells us that God wanted his people and their rulers to live godly lives. He wanted rulers to enforce godly principles. However, due to the apathy of the people and the rulers of the land, he had little choice but to destroy the land. Likewise, in today's situation, God is looking for Christians to bear the standard of God's principles. He is looking for Christians who will place godly leaders in government. Finding none, he will allow our Country to deteriorate and be destroyed.

> *³⁰ And I sought for a man among them, that should make up the hedge, and stand in the gap before me for the land, that I should not destroy it: **but I found none.***
> Ezekiel 22:30

Christians have the duty to let their lights shine. This has at least a two-fold meaning. Yes, we are to let the light of salvation shine, but we are also supposed to be allowing the light of obeying godly principles to shine as well. Ezekiel 3:16-19 speaks of the responsibility of informing the people that they are on the wrong track. It says that if that responsibility is ignored, the people will perish. Not only will the people perish but their blood will be on the hands of the ones who refused to let their light shine.

> *¹⁶ And it came to pass at the end of seven days, that the word of the L<small>ORD</small> came unto me, saying, ¹⁷ **Son of man, I have made thee a watchman unto the house of Israel: therefore hear the word at my mouth, and give them warning from me.** ¹⁸ When I say*

unto the wicked, Thou shalt surely die; and thou givest him not warning, nor speakest to warn the wicked from his wicked way, to save his life; **the same wicked man shall die in his iniquity; but his blood will I require at thine hand.** ¹⁹ *Yet if thou warn the wicked, and he turn not from his wickedness, nor from his wicked way, he shall die in his iniquity; but thou hast delivered thy soul.*

Ezekiel 3:16-19

This principle applies to today's Christians. It is our responsibility to elect godly leaders who will establish godly principles for the citizens to live by. If we, as voters, fail at our task, the blood of the ungodly citizens will be on our hands.

The greatest commandments are to love God, and love our neighbor. It is easy enough to understand that we are to love God, but far too many people are confused as to how we are to love our neighbor. Does that simply mean that we are to be kind to those we come in contact with?

{36} Master, which is the great commandment in the law? {37} Jesus said unto him, Thou shalt love the Lord thy God with all thy heart, and with all thy soul, and with all thy mind. {38} This is the first and great commandment. {39} And the second is like unto it, Thou shalt love thy neighbour as thyself. {40} On these two commandments hang all the law and the prophets.

Matt. 22:36-40

A part of letting our lights light shine has to do with espousing God's laws and principles. Matt. 5:13-16 tells us that if we do not tell the world where they are going wrong, we are worthless.

*{13} Ye are the salt of the earth: but **if the salt have lost his savour, wherewith shall it be salted? it is thenceforth good for nothing,** but to be cast out, and to be trodden under foot of men. {14} Ye are the light of the world. A city that is set on an hill cannot be hid.*

[15]Neither do men light a candle, and put it under a bushel, but on a candlestick; and it giveth light unto all that are in the house.
[16]Let your light so shine before men, that they may see your good works, *and glorify your Father which is in heaven.*
Matt. 5:13-16

Each of these Biblical references refer to our responsibility to let our moral lights shine in a dark world. Yet, we as a nation of Christians are not letting our lights shine.

There are those who claim to be Christian who justify voting for liberal (ungodly) candidates on the grounds that the liberal platform includes helping our fellow man via entitlements, hand-outs, welfare, food stamps, etc. They self-righteously point to Matt. 25:34-46 and say that voting for liberal candidates will result in obeying God's Word. After all, this passage says that if we do those things for our neighbors, we are doing them directly to God. According to liberal Christian voters, we as a nation should make the sacrifice of utilizing portions of our good fortune to help those in need.

> *34 Then shall the King say unto them on his right hand, Come, ye blessed of my Father, inherit the kingdom prepared for you from the foundation of the world: 35 For I was an hungred, and ye gave me meat: I was thirsty, and ye gave me drink: I was a stranger, and ye took me in: 36 Naked, and ye clothed me: I was sick, and ye visited me: I was in prison, and ye came unto me. 37 Then shall the righteous answer him, saying, Lord, when saw we thee an hungred, and fed thee? or thirsty, and gave thee drink? 38 When saw we thee a stranger, and took thee in? or naked, and clothed thee? 39 Or when saw we thee sick, or in prison, and came unto thee? 40 And the King shall answer and say unto them, Verily I say unto you, Inasmuch as ye have done it unto one of the least of these my*

brethren, ye have done it unto me. ⁴¹ Then shall he say also unto them on the left hand, Depart from me, ye cursed, into everlasting fire, prepared for the devil and his angels: ⁴² For I was an hungred, and ye gave me no meat: I was thirsty, and ye gave me no drink: ⁴³ I was a stranger, and ye took me not in: naked, and ye clothed me not: sick, and in prison, and ye visited me not. ⁴⁴ Then shall they also answer him, saying, Lord, when saw we thee an hungred, or athirst, or a stranger, or naked, or sick, or in prison, and did not minister unto thee? ⁴⁵ Then shall he answer them, saying, Verily I say unto you, Inasmuch as ye did it not to one of the least of these, ye did it not to me. ⁴⁶ And these shall go away into everlasting punishment: but the righteous into life eternal.

Matt. 25: 34-46

It almost sounds like the liberal Christians have a point. However, is this the proper understanding of scripture? First of all, yes, we are to help those in need. That is, as long as our act of helping others does not have the side effect of letting others know that they can engage in any sin they want to. When we vote for liberal policies of helping those in need, we are at the same time, voting for liberal policies of abortion, homosexual marriage, transgender lifestyles, etc. God's Word does not tell us that doing good in one aspect allows us to be sinful in another.

We must remember that obedience is better than sacrifice. Yes, we are to sacrifice a portion of our good fortune to help our neighbor in need, but if that sacrifice involves winking at sin, then we are doing right in the wrong way.

> *22 And Samuel said, Hath the* LORD *as great delight in burnt offerings and sacrifices, as in obeying the voice of the* LORD*?* **Behold, to obey is better than sacrifice***, and to hearken than the fat of rams. 23 For rebellion is as the sin of witchcraft, and stubbornness is as*

iniquity and idolatry. Because thou hast rejected the word of the LORD, he hath also rejected thee from being king. [24] And Saul said unto Samuel, I have sinned: for I have transgressed the commandment of the LORD, and thy words: because I feared the people, and obeyed their voice. [25] Now therefore, I pray thee, pardon my sin, and turn again with me, that I may worship the LORD. [26] And Samuel said unto Saul, I will not return with thee: for thou hast rejected the word of the LORD, and the LORD hath rejected thee from being king over Israel.

1 Sam. 15:22-26

We are to help our neighbor in need, but not at the expense of selling out all of the other godly principles.

Unfortunately, many of today's Christians are so "close to God" that they only want to pursue the winning of souls, leaving the consequences of voting to someone else. They say our job is to win souls, and everything else will take care of itself.

When Christians don't vote, or when Christians choose to vote for a liberal agenda, they are not loving their neighbor. They are self-righteous. They are Pharisees. Will God look kindly on people who had the opportunity to vote for a moral nation, but who were so self-righteous they did not do so?

Should we Vote for Conservative Values?

Liberal policies lead to the decline of a nation. Conservative policies lead to prosperity and flourishment. There can be no better example than that of the Kings of Israel and Judah. When the kings kept their eyes on God and on godly principles, the kingdom flourished. When the kings took their eyes off of God, the kingdom declined, the people suffered, the nation was plundered, and the people were taken into bondage.

Take some time to read about the leaders of the Children of Israel, and the results of their styles of leadership. Every good Hebrew king was socially conservative. They followed God, and they followed godly principles. As a result of their social conservatism, a healthy fiscal conservatism followed. When a nation is socially conservative, the nation flourishes.

On the other hand, when Hebrew kings were socially liberal (looking away from God and away from godly principles), they also suffered from a fiscal standpoint. The nation suffered from poor crops, poverty, and loss of protection from enemies. When a nation is socially liberal, the nation declines.

History is always the best teacher. We as a nation should consider a candidate's social platform first. Then, and only then, should we consider his or her financial platform. Why? Anyone can promise good financial policies, but if social liberalism is attached to the waist of those promised good financial policies, then what good can come from it? If an elected leader guides us away from God and away from godly principles, then all of the good financial policies in the whole world will not be worth the price we will have to pay for them.

The voter's first and foremost consideration should be centered on a candidate's stand on social issues. Once we determine the few contenders who pass the social test, we can move on to consider their stand on financial issues.

Why should we Vote?

Great American leaders have spoken out about our responsibility to vote, and our obligation to vote correctly. The light of godly living is hidden, or it is lifted up according to the manner in which we obey God's principles of standing up for that which is right.

"It is not easy to determine who are the more criminal. They who would make their way to places of power and trust by indirect means, or they who have so little concern for the welfare of their country as to harken to them. No civil rulers are to be obeyed when they enjoin things that are inconsistent with the commands of God: All such disobedience is lawful and glorious."

Jonathan Mayew (1720-1766) Preacher in The First Great Spiritual Awakening

When a citizen gives his suffrage [vote] to a man of known immorality he abuses his trust; he sacrifices not only his own interest, but that of his neighbor, he betrays the interest of his country."

Noah Webster (1758-1843) Father of the Dictionary & American Patriot

When you become entitled to exercise the right of voting for public officers, let it be impressed on your mind that God commands you to choose for rulers, just men who will rule in the fear of God. The preservation of [our] republican government depends on the faithful discharge of this Duty; if the citizens neglect their Duty and place unprincipled men in office, the government will soon be corrupted; laws will be made, not for the public good so much as for selfish or local purposes; corrupt or incompetent men will be appointed to execute the Laws; the public revenues will be squandered on unworthy men; and the rights of the citizen will be violated or disregarded."

Noah Webster (1758-1843) Father of the Dictionary & American Patriot

"If men of wisdom and knowledge, of moderation and temperance, of patience, fortitude and perseverance, of sobriety and true republican simplicity of manners, of zeal for the honour of the Supreme Being and the welfare of the commonwealth; if men possessed of these other excellent qualities are chosen to fill the seats of government, we may expect that our affairs will rest on a solid and permanent foundation."

Samuel Adams (1722–1803) Father of the American Revolution, Patriot and Statesman

"Bad men cannot make good citizens. It is impossible that a nation of infidels or idolaters should be a nation of freemen. It is when a people forget God, that tyrants forge their chains. A vitiated state of morals, a corrupted public conscience, is incompatible with freedom. No free

government, or the blessings of liberty, can be preserved to any people but by a firm adherence to justice, moderation, temperance, frugality, and virtue; and by a frequent recurrence to fundamental principles."

Patrick Henry (1736-1799) Patriot, Lawyer and Orator

"Republics are created by the virtue, public spirit, and intelligence of the citizens. They fall, when the wise are banished from the public councils, because they dare to be honest, and the profligate are rewarded, because they flatter the people, in order to betray them."

Joseph Story (1779-1845) Lawyer, Supreme Court Justice & influential commentators on the U.S. Constitution

"Elections belong to the people. It is their decision. If they decide to turn their back on the fire and burn their behinds, then they will just have to sit on their blisters."

Abraham Lincoln (1809–1865) Sixteenth President of the United States

"The people are responsible for the character of their Congress. If that body be ignorant, reckless, and corrupt, it is because the people tolerate ignorance, recklessness, and corruption. If it be intelligent, brave, and pure, it is because the people demand these high qualities. ... If the next centennial does not find us a great nation... it will be because those who represent the enterprise, the culture, and the morality of the nation do not aid in controlling the political forces."

James Garfield (1831-1881) Twentieth president of the United States

"America will never be destroyed from the outside. If we falter and lose our freedoms, it will be because we destroyed ourselves."

Abraham Lincoln (1809–1865) Sixteenth President of the United States

"Our nation will prosper or decline in direct proportion to our selection of leaders who are guided by the Holy Spirit. If we fail to select Godly leaders our destiny will surely be as that of the Roman Empire."

Ronald Reagan (1911-2004) 40th President of the United States

How should we Vote?

Christians should vote in every election that comes along. They should vote in the General Election; they should vote in the Primaries; they should vote in the State elections; they should vote in the County elections; they should vote in the City elections; and they should vote in the School elections.

Christians should do their homework long before the day of the election. They should study the candidates, the issues, and the questions that will show up on the ballots. Christians should obtain sample ballots prior to the Election Day so that they will know beforehand how they will vote.

The first and foremost consideration of a candidate is where that candidate stands on social issues. This information is easy to find out. A simple search on the Internet will tell you all you need to know about a candidate. Search for something like, "Social stand of candidates," and you will find a host of information about the candidates and their stand on moral issues. Select each contender, one-by-one, and read their stand on a variety of issues to help you make up your mind as to who among this vast field to consider.

Score each of the candidates on a one to ten scale, with the number one, being least like God's principles, and the number ten, being most like God's principles. Look at the candidate's stand on abortion, God in the public square, homosexual marriage, prayer in schools, etc.

Once you have picked out candidates that support godly principles, you are ready to consider their stand on financial issues. All other candidates are no longer on your list of consideration. On a one-by-one basis, consider the financial issues of candidates that you have already determined to be supporters of godly principles.

It is not that complicated. It is more related to eliminating apathy from your life than anything else. A true Christian will get out of the easy chair, research the issues, and vote for candidates who support Christian values. Then, and only then, will America begin to return to its Christian roots and become a beacon on the hill, shedding the light of godly principles to the entire world.

Endnotes

---

[1] Eighty-three percent of Americans profess to be Christian.

http://abcnews.go.com/US/story?id=90356&page=1

[2] Eighty percent of voting Evangelical Christians vote Conservative.

http://www.pewforum.org/2012/11/07/how-the-faithful-voted-2012-preliminary-exit-poll-analysis/

[3] Thirty-six percent of Evangelical Christians who are eligible to vote, do not actually vote.

http://defendchristians.org/news/the-numbers-dont-lie/

www.ingramcontent.com/pod-product-compliance
Lightning Source LLC
Chambersburg PA
CBHW050357290526
45786CB00003B/1028